*The publishers wish to acknowledge the kind assistance of
Dr Pat Morris and Mr Michael Chinery in the preparation of
this book.*

© 1976, 1982 by Grisewood & Dempsey Ltd

Designed and produced by Grisewood & Dempsey Ltd,
Elsley Court, 20-22 Great Titchfield Street, London W1

Published in 1982 in this edition by Galley Press,
an imprint of W H Smith and Son Limited
Registered No 237811 England.
Trading as WHS Distributors, St John's House,
East Street, Leicester, LE1 6NE

ISBN 0 86136 962 9

Printed and bound in Portugal by Printer Portuguesa, Sintra.

The Hedgehog

By Angela Sheehan
Illustrated by Maurice Pledger

Galley Press

For three months the hedgehog had been warm and comfortable in her underground nest. Now the weather was warmer and she had woken from her long sleep. She decided to see if the winter had really gone.

Pushing her way up through the soil to the surface, she sensed some of the other animals that shared the woodlands. Doves cooed in the trees. Pheasants were pecking in the grass. And a nesting partridge sat silent on its eggs.

The hedgehog could smell the scent of the spring flowers and the new leaves. She knew that among them there would be worms, snails, insects and lots of other good things to eat. As soon as it was dark she would be able to go out and find some food.

After such a long sleep the hedgehog felt weak and very hungry. She did not really care what she ate. Sometimes during the summer, when the cows were sleeping in the meadow, she used to go and drink milk that had trickled from their udders. But it was too far to go to the farm now. And besides the farmer might still be about.

The hedgehog snuffled around in the grass and found a slug and a centipede. Then, after a while, she found a newt. Quickly she pressed her spines into it and bit hungrily into its tasty flesh.

She went on nosing about for food but all the time she was on her guard. She had to take care that no foxes or badgers crept up on her. They were the only creatures in the wood that she really feared. Their claws and teeth were strong enough to kill a hedgehog, even if it rolled up into a ball.

But no enemies attacked the hedgehog that night. By morning she was no longer hungry but she was very tired. So she found a pile of leaves under a holly bush and, safely hidden beneath them, she settled down to sleep for the day.

For the first few days after she woke up, the hedgehog felt weary almost all the time. But soon she grew stronger and enjoyed her nightly search for food. Sometimes she caught a frog by the stream. And when she had had enough to eat and drink she found a place to sleep.

One night, as the hedgehog was eagerly tramping off to the stream, she heard a scuffling noise behind her. She stopped in her tracks and found that there was another hedgehog following her. It was a male and he wanted to mate with her.

The female took no notice of him and continued on her way. But the male hedgehog ran faster. As he came close she turned and hissed at him to make him go away.

But he did not go away. Instead, he hissed back and circled round her. She did not stop hissing, but stood very still as he continued to circle.Snorting and grunting, the hedgehog ran round and round her for almost three hours. As he came closer and closer, she grew less scared of him. And finally she allowed him to mate with her.

When they had mated the hedgehogs parted and the male went off to look for food. Just as the sun was coming up, he found a skylark's nest full of eggs. In seconds all the fragile shells were smashed and the hedgehog was greedily sucking up the creamy yolks. There was nothing the mother bird could do but fly away.

But the skylark was not the only animal that saw the hedgehog's attack. A fox saw it too. And the fox was always hungry.

As he scampered from the nest, the hedgehog caught the scent of the fox and began to run. But the fox ran too, and the hedgehog knew that he could not escape. His belly was exposed and the fox's teeth were very sharp.

Quickly the terrified hedgehog rolled up into a ball. The fox would find it hard to eat him now.

But the fox did not give up. He sniffed at the tightly rolled hedgehog and pushed it with his paw. The prickly ball began to move. The fox hit it again and this time it started to roll. Over and over it rolled, downhill towards the stream.

Suddenly, the hedgehog was in the water. He quickly unrolled himself to swim to safety – and then the fox pounced. His fangs sank into the hedgehog's belly. No spines could save him now.

Hedgehogs do not live together when they have mated as some other animals do. So the female never knew what happened to her mate. She continued to hunt for food each night and sleep during the day. And all the time a litter of young hedgehogs was growing inside her.

After about a month, the hedgehog looked for a place where she could give birth and bring up her young. She found a hole at the bottom of a stone wall and filled it with a soft bed of leaves. Safely inside, she waited for the babies to be born.

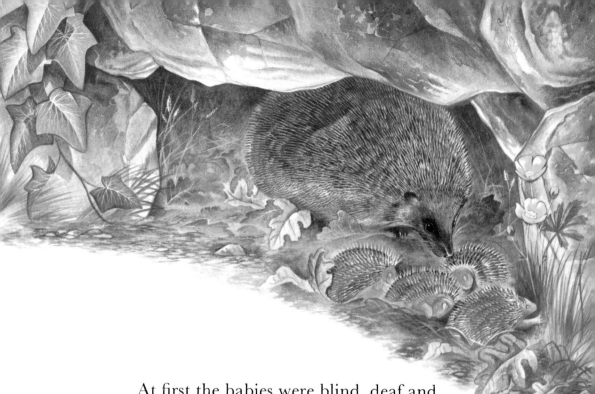

At first the babies were blind, deaf and helpless. And the white spines on their backs were quite soft. But, in about two days, a second set of harder, brown spines had grown between the soft ones. The mother hedgehog fed the babies on milk from her body. They seemed never to stop feeding and all the time they were growing and growing.

Sometimes when they were asleep, the mother hedgehog went to find food for herself. She never left them on their own for long, so she could not go far. One morning when she came back, she found that all four of the young hogs had wriggled out of the nest to take their first look at the world. But the mother knew that it was not safe for them to be outside. So, one by one, she gently gripped the scruffs of their necks in her teeth, and carried them back.

By the time the babies were about a
month old, they had grown hundreds of fine new
brown spines and a set of teeth. As soon as they
could roll up to protect themselves, their mother
took them out to find their own food. With so many
new things to eat they drank their mother's milk
less often now.

One night, later in the summer, the whole
family had a really fine feast. The young hogs ate
mostly insects and worms. But their mother found a
snake. And it was a poisonous one.

The hedgehog rushed round and round the snake as it lashed out with its poisonous fangs and tried to strike her. Then she charged at the long thin creature and it struck back at her. But, instead of killing the hedgehog, the snake got caught up in her spines.

Quickly the hedgehog rolled up, holding the neck of the snake in her mouth. Thrashing about, the snake hurt itself again and again on the hedgehog's spines. In the end, the exhausted creature fell back, dead.

Digging up worms and eating the snake had been great fun for the young hedgehogs. But, now, as they trudged home they could hardly keep their eyes open. By the time they reached the wall it was all they could do to clamber inside. They fell asleep in one large heap.

But the fox was not sleepy. He had been to the farm to catch a chicken. But the farmer had fenced in the run with barbed wire and he could not get at them. Now as he padded to the hedgehogs' nest he was very hungry. At first the fox could see only a tiny chink in the stones. But as he rooted about, one of the stones came loose.

The fox could almost see the hedgehogs
through the gap – he could certainly smell them.
The mother hedgehog was still awake. She could
feel the fox's warm breath and hear him panting.

The young hedgehogs woke up just as the fox
pressed his nose through the hole. They tried
desperately to back away from the terrifying red
face and their spines stood on end.

For a moment the mother faced the fox
bravely and snorted at the dreadful beast. But then
she rolled up to be even safer.

As long as the wall held, the great animal
could come no closer. Try though he did, the fox
could not force his way into the nest. And in the end
he went away – still hungry.

As soon as the sun went down, the mother led
the young ones from the nest. She had to find a new
place to hide them. And she had to find it quickly.
The nest in the wall might not hold out against
another attack. Without stopping to look for food,
the whole family ran silently through the woods.
Fortunately the fox was not about, and before long
they found a tree with great gnarled roots under
which they could shelter.

The young hedgehogs had grown so fast that
they would not need to stay in a nest much longer.
Their mother knew they would be safer once they
had left the nest. As the days went by, the hedgehogs
strayed farther from their mother. Soon only one of
them came back to the nest in the mornings. And
after a few days the mother drove him away. Like
the others, he must learn to look after himself.

The mother hedgehog never went back to the tree and only rarely saw her young. One morning she crossed by the badger's set. Going near the set was always dangerous, so she took no chances. Carefully, she peeped through the bracken to see that all was safe. And she saw a sight that made her prickles stand on end. A young badger had taken hold of one of her hedgehogs and was playing with him like a ball.

But she could not help him now. With luck the young badger had already eaten enough. Perhaps it would be content to enjoy its game and forget the tasty meat beneath the prickles.

Soon the summer was over. Cold winds blew and the ground was littered with berries, leaves and nuts. All the young animals had grown up and left their parents. Soon many of the birds would leave the woodlands to fly off to warmer lands where there would be plenty of food.

Gradually the woods became quieter. The buzz of insects stopped and the chorus of birds in the mornings was hardly to be heard.

As the weather grew colder all the animals began to eat more. They needed lots of fat on their bodies to see them through the cold winter.

The hedgehog ate whatever she could find. She often went out during the day now as well. She knew that there would be nothing at all to eat all the winter through.

Often the farmer's children left saucers of milk outside for the hedgehogs. The children knew how much hedgehogs love milk and their father did not like them stealing it from his cows. So early in the evening, the hedgehog would go to the edge of the farm to find the milk. Sometimes she reached the saucer only to find that the farm cats or another hedgehog had got there first and stolen all the milk. The next day she would go even earlier.

Like the dormice and the squirrels, the
hedgehog grew fatter and fatter and moved about
less and less. She did not feel strong enough to go
out and eat more food. And now food was far
harder to find.

The ground would soon be hard and the
nights were long and cold. The time had come for
the hedgehog to build her winter nest.

One night she found a good place for her nest.
There was a ditch at the bottom of an old oak tree.
And growing on the tree was a big, thick fungus.
Underneath it, the ground was dry and covered
with leaves.

The hedgehog raked the leaves into a pile with her paws and set about digging into the soil below them. Working with the sharp claws on her front paws, she moved the earth as if she were a burrowing mole.

When the hole was big enough she trampled round and round on the leaves, shuffling them with her spines into a warm lining. Then she pulled the last leaves and soil down over her and rolled into a tight ball. The soil was much warmer than the cold night air. She could sleep safely until spring.

More About Hedgehogs

A hedgehog's head

Where do Hedgehogs Live?

Hedgehogs do not live in all parts of the world. The kind of hedgehog in the story is found in most parts of Europe. It makes its home in woods and hedgerows, and even in people's gardens. Other kinds of hedgehogs live in Africa and in Asia. But there are no hedgehogs in America or Australia. The porcupine which lives in America has quills which look like big spines, but it is not related to the hedgehogs at all.

Spines and Senses

The hedgehog is about 25 centimetres (10 inches) long. It has a plump body and short legs and ears, and a tail so small that you cannot see it. Its back is covered with short, sharp spines, and its head, belly and legs are covered with hair. The hedgehog cannot see very well, but it has good ears and a sharp sense of smell. It uses its long snout to find food and sense danger.

What do Hedgehogs eat?

Hedgehogs are not fussy about their food. They can eat almost anything with their strong jaws and jagged teeth. Wild hedgehogs eat insects, earthworms, slugs, millipedes, frogs, lizards, young mice and even poisonous snakes and fruit. They feed mainly at night, rooting in the fallen leaves and litter on the ground. Their snouts and paws are so strong that they can overturn stones to get at hidden insects, and dig up worms and other tit-bits.

If a hedgehog makes its home in your garden, leave a saucer of milk for it, and you will see how much they love it. Some hedgehogs have also been known to eat baked beans, cornflakes, chocolate biscuits and custard!

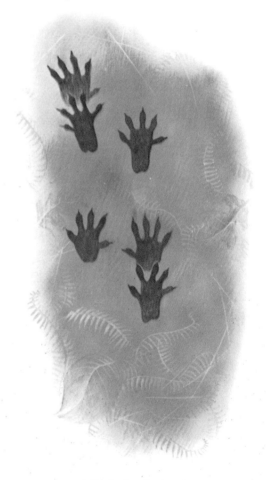

A hedgehog's tracks

Tracks and Tell-tale Signs

If you look carefully in wet mud, you can tell if a hedgehog has passed by. The hedgehog has five claws and five pads on each of its paws. Its back feet are slightly longer than the front ones, and the toes turn out. Sometimes you can also see the marks of spines outside the hedgehog's footprints. Its legs are so short that its belly often touches the ground and the spines on its back drag in the mud.

Other signs that you can see are broken dung heaps and piles of rubbish that have been disturbed. Hedgehog droppings are small black pellets with rounded ends. They usually contain the remains of insects.

Is it True?

Many stories have been told about hedgehogs and nobody knows whether they are true or not. Some people laugh at farmers for believing that hedgehogs steal milk from cows, but other people say they have seen them sucking milk from their udders.

Everyone knows that hedgehogs steal eggs from birds. But do they also spear apples and strawberries on their spines and carry them away? The picture below was drawn long, long ago. It shows some hedgehogs rolling on their backs under apple trees, so that their spines stick into the fallen fruit. Few people today have ever seen a hedgehog doing this, but many people believe that they do.

Foam Bath

One mystery about hedgehogs has never been explained. Many people have seen hedgehogs 'anointing' themselves. They lick an object with their tongues until they froth at the mouth. Then they rear up on their front legs and twist their heads around to smear the foam on their spines. Sometimes they twist so hard that they topple right over. Scientists cannot think of any reason why they anoint themselves. But perhaps one day they will find out.

An old picture of hedgehogs stealing apples